Original title:
The Ocean's Reflection

Copyright © 2025 Creative Arts Management OÜ
All rights reserved.

Author: William Hawthorne
ISBN HARDBACK: 978-1-80587-349-5
ISBN PAPERBACK: 978-1-80587-819-3

bi n h nh phúc

When waves wave back with a cheeky grin,
Seagulls look down, oh, where to begin?
Surfboards tumbling, laughter in the air,
Splashing a crab, does it even care?

Flip-flops flying, on toes they land,
Sandcastles built, like dreams that stand.
A mermaid giggles, her tail's on the loose,
No fish to catch, just a party truce!

Sunsets paint hues of jellybean bright,
As we dance 'neath the stars with all our might.
The tide tosses jokes, a playful spree,
With every wave, we laugh with glee!

So raise a soda, make a toast with cheer,
To the silly sea life, let's give a cheer!
For in this wet wonder, we truly see,
Joy splashes wildly, just like you and me!

Solitude's Serenade in Aqua

A fish in a bowler hat, quite grand,
Sips tea with a crab who can barely stand.
They gossip of tides and who's pulling each fin,
While seaweed does yoga, trying to fit in.

A dolphin with shades, quite the suave fellow,
Sings songs to the shells with a voice quite mellow.
The seagulls pull pranks, with a caw that's a tease,
While barnacles chuckle, all stuck at their knees.

Passing Clouds Over Still Waters

Clouds float by like marshmallows above,
While turtles play poker, a game they all love.
With a wink and a nod, they bluff with great flair,
While seahorses giggle, claiming they're rare.

The sun starts to set, and the waves play a tune,
As crabs dance a jig under the light of the moon.
The starfish tap toes to a soft, sandy beat,
While flounders break dance with their moves so sweet.

Meditations of the Sea Breeze

A seaweed guru sits calm on a rock,
Teaching fish yoga, quite the shocking talk.
They stretch and they twist, with fins in delight,
While laughter erupts like a wave in the night.

A clam offers pearls, wearing shades for the sun,
Claims each one's a secret for having some fun.
Jellyfish waltz in their translucent grace,
While waves roll along, splashing foam on their face.

Tidal Musings in the Evening Light

As the tide rolls in, the otters are wise,
With their playful antics beneath brightening skies.
They juggle sea balls and float on their backs,
While seagulls inquire about fashionable snacks.

The twilight brings forth a parade of the rays,
Each fish in a coat, showing off in arrays.
They giggle and shimmer, all colors collide,
As laughter unites in this watery ride.

Where Stars Meet the Sea

Stars tangle their lights, in waves of delight,
Fishes wear shades, in the moon's soft bite.
A crab throws a party, with a dance so spry,
Seagulls make jokes, as they swoop and fly.

Waves whisper secrets, in a giggly tone,
A dolphin just snorted, in a seaweed throne.
Beach balls go bouncing, with unexpected grace,
While starfish all cheer, in their sandy space.

Mists of the Mind

Fog rolls in slow, like a sleepy surprise,
Mermaids are yawning, with sleep in their eyes.
A clam tells a tale, but it's hard to believe,
He swears it was gold, then he starts to grieve.

Buoys are just bobbing, with a sock on their head,
A bench-warm crab plays, he's too cool to dread.
The breeze carries giggles, from out on the shore,
While seagulls are squawking, 'We've heard it before!'

Secrets of Sand and Surf

Sandy toes wiggle, like they've lost the plot,
While shells share gossip, in a sunbaked spot.
A flounder is laughing, beneath his sea guise,
While jellyfish float by, with a wave and surprise.

Surfboards act silly, surfing bubbles and bliss,
As sea turtles tumble, in a salty abyss.
Each wave is a joker, with pranks to deploy,
And the tide just cackles, 'Aren't we a joy?'

Celestial Waters

Stars take a dive, flipping with a whirl,
While fish join the fun, with each little twirl.
A shark sings a tune, though it's off-key and loud,
While octopuses laugh, forming quite the crowd.

Clouds get confused, swirling all around,
Crabs mimic astronauts, on the soft ground.
The tide rolls in boisterous, like a slapstick show,
As laughter keeps rising, with each ebb and flow.

Underneath the Whispering Skies

Bubbles rise with a giggle,
A fish in a tie, looking slick,
Turtles break dance on the surface,
While crabs throw a conga, oh what a kick!

Seagulls gossip with a flair,
Their beaks sharp, but hearts of cheese,
The dolphins play tag in the air,
As jellyfish float with grace and ease.

A whale belts out a tune,
To the rhythm of a surfboard's glide,
Where seaweed sways like a ballerina,
And starfish vye for the spotlight with pride.

Clownfish chuckle, what a sight,
With anemones tickling, giggling loud,
Underneath this silly blight,
Every wave, a laughter shroud.

Reverberations of the Nautilus

Nautilus rides a wave of cheer,
With a shell that sparkles so bright,
He spins in circles, sheds a tear,
For the shrimp that tried to dance all night.

Octopus plays cards with the sun,
His poker face, one for the books,
But with eight arms it's hardly fair fun,
He wins all the bets with sly looks.

Starfish critique the latest style,
Comparing spots, and arms with flair,
They judge the waves, stay for a while,
And giggle over who pulls a stare.

With conch shells blaring jokes galore,
Each burp echoes like a bubble,
As sea cucumbers roll on the floor,
In salty delight over their trouble.

Haikus of the Deep Blue

Fish with silly hats,
Swim in circles, laugh and splash,
Bubbles pop like dreams.

A crab takes a walk,
Sideways on a sandcastle,
Sandy throne in sight.

Seaweed sways and sways,
Tickling fins beneath the waves,
Whales hum goofy tunes.

Driftwood holds a chat,
With a lost flip-flop nearby,
What a pair they make!

Symphony of the Endless Horizon

In a concert of waves,
Drumsticks made of seaweed,
Clams sing soprano, oh brave,
As whales join in with heed.

Seashells play the flute,
While tetras jive on the floor,
A spray of fun takes root,
As krill cheer them evermore.

Mollusks bust a move,
Under the spotlight of foam,
With glistening grooves,
They celebrate in their home.

Under the sun's embrace,
They twirl in laughter, so spry,
In this salty space,
All share a giggle and sigh.

Waters of Whimsy

Bubbles rise with a giggling sound,
Seagulls dance, swirling around.
Fish wear hats, oh what a sight,
As mermaids join in pure delight.

Sandy castles, not too grand,
Collapse with laughter, like a band.
Crabs wearing sunglasses, strut at ease,
Jellyfish float, they aim to please.

Waves crash down with a hearty cheer,
Shells hide tales of fun each year.
Turtles waddle, trying to race,
Dolphins laughing, keeping pace.

With every splash, a chuckle flies,
As sunbeams peek from fluffy skies.
Salty air fills with blissful scenes,
What a life, with ocean dreams!

Beneath the Sky's Canvas

Clouds sail by, a parade of fluff,
Seashells giggle, that's quite enough.
Starfish pose like rockstars, bold,
Their glittering forms, a sight to behold.

Paddling ducks play a silly game,
While octopuses dance, never the same.
Surfboards tumble, what a mess,
But laughter bubbles, we must confess.

Kites tickle breeze, a playful affair,
As flip-flops fly through salty air.
Little feet sprint, chasing the tide,
With joy in hearts, and no need to hide.

Painted skies as the sunset glows,
Tickled by waves, where laughter flows.
Every ripple echoes their cheer,
As day ends, we gather near.

Depths of Introspection

Beneath the waves, a deep sea quest,
Fish ponder life, with scales well-dressed.
A turtle thinks, what's really true?
And a clownfish wonders, who's who?

Down in the reef, a starfish sighs,
Contemplating all the fishy lies.
Lost in thoughts, the sea cucumbers float,
While seaweed whispers, 'Just rock the boat!'

Anemones giggle, in soft green beds,
While squid doodle with their wiggly heads.
Crabs with glasses, reading sea scrolls,
In this underwater world, who knows?

Philosophers swimming in ocean's embrace,
Finding the meaning, at a slow pace.
With each wave, insights are set free,
Silly musings of deep-sea glee!

Serene Solitude

On a quiet shore, with no cares in mind,
Seashells remind us of treasures we find.
A lone penguin slides down the sand,
With a belly flop, oh isn't life grand?

A beach ball bounces, off a crab's head,
With each little giggle, a splash of red.
Sandcastles stand, but not for too long,
As waves give a nudge; they must move along.

Starfish sunbathe, on rocks so warm,
While curious gulls bring about a charm.
Laughter erupts in this calm retreat,
As nature's joy becomes quite a feat.

Sipping lemonade under a palm,
With a breeze that carries a whisper of calm.
In the stillness, humor finds a way,
To dance and twirl, brightening our day.

A Symphony of Salt and Sun

Waves play the ukulele, so bright,
Seagulls dance like they're taking flight.
Crabs shake it on the sandy floor,
Clams clap along, they can't ignore.

Bikini-clad folks try to surf,
Falling face-first, oh what a smurf!
A sandcastle towers, a noble feat,
Until a dog thinks it's a treat!

Sunbathers roast like marshmallows,
While sunscreen fights the sneaky fellows.
Chairs blow away like they've lost their mind,
Funny how the beach can be so unkind!

With a splash and a laugh, we run and play,
Who knew the sea would steal the day?
From flippers to floats, we all have fun,
This salty life, oh, how it's begun!

Illusions of the Abyss

Fish wearing hats, oh what a sight,
Swimming through coral, day and night.
They gossip of humans, clumsy and loud,
While bubbles float up; they're snickering proud.

An octopus juggles with slippery flair,
While a whale decides to dye its hair.
Mermaids giggle at our sinking boats,
As they sip tea from their fancy coats.

A dolphin flips, then takes a bow,
Says, 'You think you're great? Try this now!'
I tried to dance, but tripped on a fin,
The spectacle sure made all the fish grin.

With laughter echoing 'neath the sea waves,
I wondered if they'd learned how to behave.
These underwater antics are quite a twist,
Who knew that deep down, fun can exist?

Horizon's Embrace

With the sunset blush, they all come out,
Flip-flop army ready, no hint of doubt.
Ice cream drips, a sticky affair,
Seagulls swoop in for their share!

Sandy toes and salty hair,
A beach ball flies without a care.
Kids chase waves, slipping on their fate,
The tide rolls in—watch out, it's late!

The sunset paints the sky like a joke,
As laughter erupts from a nearby folk.
Someone screams, 'Don't go near that pool!'
Only to find it's an empty cooler, how cool!

Endless giggles at the ocean's edge,
We swear we'll be wise, but then we pledge.
Fun in the sun, till daylight's gone,
As stars appear, the laughter goes on!

Shades of Tranquility

Sipping coconut water with a grin,
While floats parade like they're on the tin.
Umbrellas shade my sunburnt skin,
But the towel war is where I begin!

With dogs surfing on waves, what a sight,
Cartwheeling shells, chasing the light.
Sunburnt picnic, all flavors abound,
Until the ants lead me where they're found.

Collecting seashells, a collector's dream,
A superstar crab struts in my scheme.
"Don't take my home!" it shrieks with a cheer,
But really, I just wanted a souvenir!

This quiet place, but oh, what glee,
With giggles carried by the salty spree.
Laughter painted on the canvas bright,
In these moments of calm, we find delight!

A Wave's Silent Song

A wave once tried to sing a tune,
But sloshed its notes to the moon.
It splashed and laughed, lost its pitch,
Gurgles of joy, a watery glitch.

Seagulls perched, rolling their eyes,
Wondering how a wave could devise.
With each foamy burst, it danced with glee,
A soggy singer, proud and free.

Shells joined in with a clap of shells,
The horizon chuckled, casting spells.
As bubbles rose with a hiccup sound,
A symphony of fun, most profound.

The salty breeze blew a cheeky jest,
Who knew the sea could be so blessed?
With splashes loud, the sea took flight,
Waves in concert, what a sight!

Dreams Adrift in Blue.

Riding high on a floaty dream,
Fish wear shades, basking in sunbeam.
A jellyfish grins with a squishy sway,
While dolphins giggle, they surf and play.

Mermaids braid their hair with seaweed,
Turning tides answer every need.
"You missed a spot!" a clam suddenly quips,
As sea turtles roll their watery lips.

Clouds overhead formed a sleepy cat,
Who snores gently, gone flat as a mat.
A crab crawls by with a funny strut,
His shadow feels like a giant nut.

In this azure realm of endless fun,
Even the starfish dance, one by one.
Each wave's a smile, splashing bright,
In dreams adrift, joy takes flight!

Whispers of the Tides

Whispers float with the ocean breeze,
Jokes exchanged between swift sea wees.
"Why did the fish blush?" it teased so sly,
"Because it saw the ocean's net, oh my!"

Every ripple laughed, every splash cheered,
Salty secrets, no one feared.
Crabs painted nails, quite the show,
While barnacles chimed in with the flow.

An octopus juggled with eight wobbly arms,
While sea cucumbers flashed their charms.
"Be careful!" warned the wise old mackerel,
"Too much jiggle can lose you your skeletal."

As twilight approached and the waves grew tame,
The sea's laughter echoed, calling your name.
Under starlit skies, the tides still abide,
Whispers of cheer, in the currents they glide.

Echoes Beneath the Surface

Bubbles are giggles beneath the blue,
As fish throw a party, just for a few.
A grouper brought snacks, what a delight,
Pricey sea urchins, they had a bite!

The octopus was DJ, spinning fast,
With tentacles wiggling, making it last.
Snails grooved low while shrimp took a chance,
Dancing along, they all joined the dance.

A narwhal trumpeted with a whistle,
As angelfish sparkled, their fins a twinkle.
"Shh! Listen close!" the eel gave a shout,
Echoes of laughter chased worries out.

In the depths where the sunlight fades,
Joy can be found in the dance parades.
With creatures so quirky, how could it be,
Nothing but laughter beneath the sea?

Echoing Silences in the Blue

A fish waved hello from afar,
With a grin that could light a bazaar.
He tried to tell jokes, but they fell flat,
As a seaweed-wrapped cat took a nap.

The crabs danced like they lost their shell,
While seagulls laughed, saying, "Oh, swell!"
One clam shouted, "I'm not very bold,
But I still want a story—preferably sold!"

Bubbles popped like forgotten dreams,
As dolphins played with their gleaming beams.
They juggled starfish and sparkled with glee,
Till a turtle yelled, "Hey! Save one for me!"

With a splash and a dash, they all set sail,
The sea's silly follies told a tall tale.
As the sunset painted the water bright,
They danced through the waves, what a sight!

A Tidal Tale

Once a whale sought a grand ballet,
But tripped on a seal in a playful fray.
He flopped and he floundered, what a sight!
Even the barnacles giggled in delight.

Fish in tuxedos swam with flair,
While jellyfish floated without a care.
They formed a conga line by the shore,
And even the octopus begged for more.

The tide pulled back, but it couldn't resist,
The urge to join this splashing twist.
As the sun dipped low, and the stars arose,
The sea held a party, in fancy repose.

"Let's toast with some kelp!" shouted a clam,
As they laughed 'til the night turned to jam.
What a tidal wave of joy we made,
With a rhythm and cheer that will never fade!

Amidst the Waves' Embrace

In the shallows, a sea sponge sang,
While starfish clapped, and the dolphins rang.
Anemones tickled their squishy friends,
As laughter echoed where the sea extends.

A crab tried to dance, oh what a show,
With two left claws, but he'd steal the glow.
The other critters cheered with mirth,
As he performed with great hint of girth.

Drifting along, a shipwrecked shoe,
Brought tales of adventure, both silly and true.
Fishes flipped and flopped their fins,
Encouraging treasure hunts full of wins.

As twilight crept in with a wink,
The mermaids joined in, ready to link.
They twirled through currents under the moon,
Creating waves of giggles, oh so soon!

Skimming the Surface of Dreams

A dolphin dreamed of a flying spree,
While pondering how she'd fit in a tree.
With a flip and a splash, she took to the air,
Only to land on a whale's fuzzy hair.

The jellyfish floated, glowing quite bright,
Proposing a dance under the soft moonlight.
They wiggled with glee, an underwater funk,
While winks from a grouper sunk the ship's trunk.

From the seaweed, a crab sent a wave,
"Dinner's ready! Come on, be brave!"
But they found out too late, it was just a joke,
As they each held a fork and laughed till they broke.

So beneath the waves, should you listen close,
You'll hear laughter where the fish all do boast.
From prancing shrimp to a starfish's tap,
The ocean hums with a funny old rap!

Nature's Canvas at Dawn

Colors splash as daylight breaks,
Seagulls laugh at fish that wakes.
The sky's a joke, a canvas bright,
Where clouds play tag and squawk with might.

Turtles dance in quite a spin,
While crabs wear hats, oh where to begin?
They strut down sand like they own the lease,
Chasing sunbeams that never cease.

Sandcastles lean, eager to fall,
As kids hoot loud, and seagulls call.
With buckets and shovels, they dig a fate,
For deep-sea treasures that won't await.

The water knits a funny sweater,
With flip-flops tangled, the sun's a debtor.
Giggles bounce on rippling foam,
In this silly place, we all call home.

Loops of Salt and Solitude

Salt shakers laugh on the lunchroom floor,
As seagulls eye fries, they always score.
The waves wiggle, 'Is it lunchtime yet?'
While beach balls bounce like a marionette.

A stingray drifts, quite the charmer,
It flirts with fish, 'I'm a real swimmer!'
With every splash, they giggle and tease,
These aquatic games will surely please.

A crab wears shades, looking quite cool,
While starfish claim, 'We've got the pool!'
The ocean's the party, all here in suits,
With flip-flops poppin' like silly boots.

Drifting away on tides of glee,
Even the tide gets silly, you see!
In this loop of laughter and salty dreams,
The sea's a jester, bursting at the seams.

Mirrors of the Infinite Sea

Waves giggle as they flip and roll,
Reflecting jokes that made them whole.
The dolphins leap, they're in on the fun,
Synchronized swims where two become one.

The sun's a clown, wearing sunglasses wide,
Belly flops in waves; it takes a ride.
Fish play peek-a-boo in coral dens,
'Catch me if you can!' they tease their friends.

Barnacles cling, gossip in code,
While sea cucumbers dance, off the road.
They throw a party deep in the blue,
Where laughter bubbles and joy feels new.

Sand dollars twirl, what a sight to behold,
While waves whisper secrets never told.
In a mirror of camaraderie, all unite,
As the sea reflects joy, pure delight.

A Refuge Between Waves

A shorebird squawks, 'Hey, come join me!'
While crabs do the cha-cha, skipping free.
Shells are taking bets on who can dive,
As the seafoam tickles, it's quite the jive.

Flip-flop fashion contests start anew,
It's a runway show for the sea's debut.
With barnacles judging and seaweed cheers,
Laughing waves bring joy through the years.

Beach towels spread, a laughter brigade,
Where sand angels giggle, unafraid.
As waves swish by, and banter flows,
Finding solace in the funny, who knows?

From jellyfish jokes to seal's whoopee,
The fun flows endless, like a wild spree.
In this refuge where giggles collide,
Each bubble that bursts brings joy alongside!

Glistening Beneath Whispers

Bubbles giggle as they rise,
A fish tells jokes beneath the skies.
Seagulls cackle, join the fun,
They dive for fries, then they run.

A crab with friends makes silly shapes,
Dancing clumsily in gappy capes.
They stumble over seaweed's hold,
A sight to see, so brave, so bold.

A dolphin leaps with a cheeky grin,
Splashing waves, let the laughter begin!
He flips and flops without a care,
The sun just chuckles, warms the air.

In this watery world of joy and cheer,
Every splash brings another ear to hear.
With every wave a giggle unfolds,
Nature's punchlines are worth their gold.

A Voyage in Tranquil Waters

Sailing forth on a jellyfish boat,
With sea cucumbers offering to float.
The captain's a squid, lost in his map,
As starfish giggle, 'Just take a nap!'

Waves tickle the hull with a gentle tease,
And crabs in chairs munching on cheese.
A turtle drifts by, all chill and slow,
Saying, 'Hurry up, mate! Where's the show?'

Bubbles bursting, giggly pops,
Our anchor's a fish who really just flops.
As dolphins hold a talent show,
Their mermaid fans sing, "Way to go!"

The voyage goes on with laughter and fun,
We'll sail till sunset, till day is done.
In peaceful waters, the jokes never cease,
Each moment floats, a buoyant lease.

The Silent Call of Sirens

Siren songs echo, sweetly bizarre,
But they're just singing to fish in a jar.
Each note drips laughter, a mystical tease,
Inviting clams to join in with ease.

They comb through seaweed with glimmers of glee,
While trying to avoid a very big flea.
The mermaids trip over their glittery tails,
As the tide carries whispers of their curvy trails.

With sea otters cheerfully rolling along,
They join the mad tune, a chaotic song.
Bubbles pop out, like notes in the air,
Making fish giggle without a care.

In aquatic realms where mirth takes its rise,
The quietest calls often bring the best highs.
A splash, a flounder, a tickling wave,
Each moment is magic—how funny, how brave!

Fragments of Forgotten Shores

Sandy castles lose their crowns with a roar,
As waves come crashing on the playful shore.
Children join in, launching wet sand,
While crabs retreat, scuttling on land.

Seashells giggle, 'Remember that time?'
When dolphins juggled and made sunsets rhyme?
A lighthouse chuckles while keeping the score,
'Wink twice for safety and add even more!'

Beach balls bounce, a party so bright,
Seagulls drop snacks, what a silly sight!
Laughter echoes as sandcastles topple,
Consequences of that wild beach shuffle.

These fragments of laughter, lost in the tide,
Are tales of fun that the waves can't hide.
With each rolling crest, our joy's in the air,
Creating memories for all who dare.

Silhouettes Against the Sea

The seagulls squawk with flair,
While beach balls soar through air.
Fried fish do the cha-cha dance,
As clumsy crabs take a chance.

Sunbathers lost in their own style,
Under umbrellas, they rest a while.
A dog steals a towel, runs for fun,
Making everyone laugh in the sun.

Waves crash with a thunderous joke,
As sandcastles vanish, it's no hoax.
The tide rolls in, giggling quite loud,
While flip-flops scatter, a clumsy crowd.

And as the day begins to fade,
A clown fish honks, in a playful parade.
They swim and splash, without a care,
In this seaside circus, beyond compare.

Mirage of the Water's Edge

A mirage winks with a silly grin,
Where mermaids play and toaster spins.
Fish with sunglasses strut about,
Making splashes with a cheerful shout.

A message in a bottle, what could it be?
Just a note that says, 'Where's my tea?'
Seashells gossip under the sun,
As dolphins plan their next big run.

A lobster juggles friends on the shore,
While octopuses dance in a shopping store.
Turtles spin in their own ballet,
Wearing party hats, loving the day.

And when the sun dips low for a nap,
There's laughter around, a joyful clap.
The coast is filled with whimsy bright,
Under the stars, they share delight.

Dreams on Salted Breezes

On salted winds, dreams take flight,
While jellyfish glow in the moonlight.
Seagulls play tag, oh what a sight,
Squawking their plans, from morning to night.

A crab tells tales of summer fun,
Of treasure maps and silly runs.
He trips on sand, then roars with glee,
As the starfish join in jubilee.

Waves whisper secrets, giggle and flow,
As children build castles, row by row.
But watch out now, as a wave sneaks in,
Turning a kingdom into a din!

And in the twilight, a boat sails by,
With fanciful fish that jump and fly.
They dance in circles with gleeful cheer,
Beneath a moonlit sky, oh so dear!

Shimmering Secrets in the Currents

In shimmering waves, secrets are known,
A fish sings songs of the laughter grown.
With a flip and a splash, they share a tale,
Of a sunken shoe and a timid whale.

Octopuses plot, with eight arms in tow,
Dancing in circles, stealing the show.
Clam chowder dreams float by in the sun,
While the starfish giggles, oh what fun!

A dock filled with laughter, a parrot squawks loud,
As barnacles chuckle, forming a crowd.
The sharks tell jokes that they just can't keep,
While dolphin friends giggle, rolling in sleep.

As evening arrives, in a glow of delight,
The coastline is painted with laughter so bright.
With every wave that crashes and plays,
Saltwater joy turns into a haze.

Dreamscapes on Water

A fish wore a hat, quite the sight,
He danced in the waves, full of delight.
The seagulls all laughed, what a scene,
As he twirled in the surf, looking quite keen.

In the depths, a crab plays it cool,
Sporting sunglasses, he thinks he's a fool.
With a pinch and a pose, he strikes a grand show,
While the starfish just rolls, taking it slow.

A dolphin swam by, with a flip and a twist,
Shouting, "I'm the best, how can you resist?"
But the turtles just sighed, moving at snail pace,
As they watched the show with a sleepy embrace.

A buoy with a grin bobbed up and down,
Passing fish teased, "What a goofy clown!"
As waves roared with laughter, the sea joined in,
This funny parade, where all could just win.

Reflections of Distant Shores

A crab with a camera snapped away,
Catching selfies at noon, what a bright day!
He posed with a fish, in a comical grin,
While the waves crashed around with a bubbly spin.

A clam opened wide, just to have fun,
Saying, "I'm the star, watch my pearls run!"
But the sand made a joke, whispered so sly,
"Close your shell, dear friend, the tide's passing by!"

A dolphin taught seagulls how to dive,
But they flapped and they flailed, struggling to thrive.
With flippers turned clumsy, they made quite a splash,
As fishes all giggled, "This ain't no gash!"

In the breeze, the waves sang a silly tune,
Swaying to rhythms beneath the bright moon.
With laughter and giggles, all creatures unite,
In this grand, watery world, pure delight.

Chasing Dusk on the Tide

As sunbeams dipped low, a crab grabbed a shell,
He dressed it in glitter and rang his bell.
"Come see my new bling!" he shouted with glee,
While fishes just laughed, "Oh, look at that spree!"

A starfish was stuck, on a rock quite bizarre,
He called for a friend, "Bring a rental car!"
But all that flowed by were seashells and sand,
"Guess I'll wait for tide's help; that was the plan!"

A mirage appeared, it was just a fat seal,
He bobbed with a grin, yelling, "What a steal!"
But the shrimp threw confetti, dancing around,
"Party time now, let us revel unbound!"

The twilight's embrace brought giggles and cheer,
In this wild, splashy place, filled with friendly gear.
As the waves whispered secrets, the laughter took flight,
Chasing shadows together, into the night!

Calls from the Coral

A fish sent a postcard from under the sea,
"Wish you were here, it's so much fun, whee!"
He talked of the bubbles, and how they all sang,
While dolphins did flips, a hilarious gang.

A sea turtle snored, while the others all danced,
With each silly move, the whole reef got pranced.
The octopus laughed, he spun in a twist,
As colors swirled round, "Hey, you get the gist?"

A clam threw a party, shells decked neat and clean,
With bright party hats, it was quite the scene.
But a starfish tripped, oh what a blunder,
As everyone giggled, the waves rumbled thunder!

In the coral's embrace, they all found their fun,
With laughter and antics, no need to outrun.
As tides floated secrets from far away lands,
These calls from the depths made us all understand!

Ebbing Moments of Reflection

Waves crash and giggle, they tease the shore,
Seagulls squawk jokes, we all beg for more.
Sandcastles crumble, a grand sandy feat,
The tide rolls away, oh, where's my cool seat?

Mermaids are sunbathing, don't they look fine?
They wave at the sun, sipping seaweed wine.
Fish flash their scales, fancy but shy,
I throw in a line—wait, was that a pie?

Finding treasure chests, but all I get's shells,
The clams are all laughing; they know all the tells.
Jellyfish're dancing, in quite the craze,
I wish I could join, but I feel out of phase.

As the sun dips low, the shadows roll wide,
My beach ball takes off—a wild, fun ride.
Chasing it down, I trip on my toes,
Next time I'll stick to just watching it doze.

Frayed Edges of Dusk

The sun yawns slowly, a big orange ball,
It's losing its grip, fair warning to all.
Waves whisper secrets, but what do they mean?
Seagull leads yoga, all calm and serene.

Each grain of sand is a joke that it knows,
Crabs juggle shells while the sunset glows.
Fish wear top hats, swimming with flair,
They're off to a gala, but I'm still stuck here.

Spotting a dolphin, he winks with a splash,
Making waves of laughter, oh, how they clash!
Starfish in bowties are dancing tonight,
I don't have shoes, but I'm feeling alright!

With each laugh that rolls, the tide ebbs away,
Fishing for humor at the end of the day.
As night finally falls, the stars start to peep,
The ocean's humor, too strong for sleep.

Flotsam of Melancholy Thoughts

In the tide's embrace, lost dreams float about,
A rubber duck's pondering what life's about.
Sun hats and sunglasses, all washed ashore,
They giggle and gossip of days gone before.

Drifting on currents, a small child's toy,
Once so beloved, now lacking much joy.
Starfish share stories of hope and despair,
While sea cucumbers just don't seem to care.

A sandy old crab, with a frown on his face,
Has lost his way home, it's a lonesome place.
The tide gives a wink, then rolls in with sand,
"All that's flotsam's just part of the plan!"

Yet laughter still bubbles from bubbles in flight,
Their giggles remind us, it's all to be light.
So we gather our treasures, with hearts full of cheer,
Melancholy's just jokes that we mishear.

Caressing the Horizon's Edge

At dawn's soft blush, the waves start to play,
Shells whisper sweet nonsense, come join the buffet!
The sun smiles wide, with a wink in the sky,
I wave back and trip, oh my, oh my!

Mirth is contagious on this sandy expanse,
Starfish in tuxedos invite us to dance.
A dolphin high-fives with a splash and a dive,
Is this a circus? I feel so alive!

Crabs in a conga line take center stage,
While clams drop the beat, breaking all the cage.
Their rhythm is catchy; I can hardly stay still,
Catching the groove is quite the thrill!

As stars wink goodbye and the daylight comes clear,
We'll bottle this joy like fine ocean beer.
Today was a blast, full of laughter and glee,
If only the sun would stay here with me!

Ripples of Time

The waves giggle as they crash,
Sipping snacks, they make a splash.
Seagulls in their funny hats,
Count the fish like silly rats.

Tides do tango, moon's their guide,
Slippers on, the crabs all slide.
Starfish ponder, lost in thought,
Did they order what they ought?

Shells are busy on the sand,
Playing poker, isn't that grand?
Time drifts by in frothy fun,
Who knew the beach could make you run?

So let's dance with each new wave,
Laughter's a treasure, let's be brave.
As we surf through this light rhyme,
Let's cherish these ripples of time.

Lullabies of the Deep

In the deep where fish do snore,
Surfers sleep on ocean floor.
Crabs are strumming on the strings,
Making music, oh what flings!

Seashells hum a silly tune,
Jellyfish dance like a balloon.
Octopus in pajamas tight,
Claims he's ready for the night.

Bubbles blow up in a line,
Squids are drawing doodles fine.
Waves will rise to sing along,
In this world where fish belong.

Laughter echoes through the tide,
Every wave's a joyful ride.
As we sway in deep sea's keep,
Let's drift away on lullabies deep.

Beneath a Canvas of Waves

Under waves where colors mix,
Fish wear glasses and do tricks.
Starfish painting with their feet,
Creating art that's quite a feat.

Corals gossip with a flair,
Bubbling stories, leaving care.
Whales juggle cool pearls with ease,
While sea turtles share some cheese.

Seas are canvas, bright and bold,
With tales of treasures waiting to be told.
Crabs roll by in rainbow hues,
Whistling tunes as they peruse.

So dive in and join the spree,
In this art where all are free.
With laughter echoing like raves,
Let's celebrate beneath the waves.

Secrets Held in Coral Reefs

Coral castles filled with jest,
Fish play hide-and-seek, the best.
Anemones wave with a grin,
Inviting all to jump right in.

Seahorses with little ties,
Making waves, oh what a rise!
Clownfish telling silly jokes,
While sea urchins act like folks.

At twilight, dolphins join the dance,
Wiggling fins, they take the chance.
Secrets shared in silly squeaks,
As seaweed sways and giggles peaks.

And under stars so bright and clear,
Lies laughter that we all hold dear.
With each wave crashing, a new release,
Secrets bloom in a sea of peace.

Nautical Reverie

A crab in a hat, what a sight,
Dancing with fish, what a delight.
Seagulls cawing, 'Join the fun!'
While starfish glare at the baking sun.

A whale with a smile, so grand,
Spinning in circles, it's quite the band.
Turtles race with their shells so slick,
Who knew they were all up for a trick?

Octopus jokes, a real hoot,
Tickling fish with a slippery boot.
Bubbles burst with laughter, oh my,
Under the waves, they giggle and sigh.

The surf plays tunes, crabs start to groove,
Each splash and wave adjusts the move.
So come join this splashy parade,
Where funny sea tales are happily made.

Celestial Ripples

Once in a tide, there's a tale so bright,
A dolphin disco under the moonlight.
With fins in the air and a splashy twist,
Even the jellyfish can't help but assist.

Starfish forming a conga line,
Low tide is ample for dancing divine.
A buoy with tunes, it's the anchor's role,
Keeping the rhythm, heart and soul.

Seashells chuckle at the jokes they hear,
Seaweed sways, oh so near.
The sun peeks in, catching a glimpse,
Of mermaids giggling in flippy swims.

Bubbles bouncing to an ocean beat,
Turtles rolling, oh what a feat!
Life beneath the waves, a playful sight,
With laughter and giggles, all feels just right.

Whispers of the Waves

A clam with a secret, what could it be?
Whispering tales of fishy jubilee.
The surf giggles, tickling the shore,
While crabs take selfies, oh where's the door?

Mermaids practicing their best silly pose,
One flips her tail, and over she goes!
A starfish sighs, 'This isn't my day,'
As he rolls in the sand, what can I say?

Lobsters laughing, telling tall tales,
Of adventurous trips on magical gales.
Bubbles float by, with glee they sway,
The ocean's chuckle brightens up the day.

Seagulls join in with their wacky songs,
Chasing fish under water where each one belongs.
So dive in the fun, don't let it cease,
In this salty realm where we find our peace.

Meditations in Motion

Fish in a line, practicing yoga,
Downward fish and a prawn doing a toga.
Waves chant mantras, they crash and they roll,
While crabs find balance on a wobbly shoal.

A snail in a race, what a sight to see,
Taking his time, as slow as can be.
But here comes a flounder, all quick and spry,
"Oh dear, why did I even try?"

With seaweed stretching in every direction,
It's a training day full of affection.
The ocean's mood, like a rollercoaster ride,
Keeps us all laughing, with currents as guide.

A sea cucumber joins with a wiggle and plop,
"To meditate, you don't have to stop!"
So let's gather 'round for a chuckle or two,
In this watery world where mirth shines through.

Reflections in a Glassy Tide

A seagull landed with a thud,
It slipped and skidded in the mud.
With a squawk that echoed wide,
He rolled like a log on an ocean slide.

Fish wearing sunglasses just to tease,
Flipping their tails with such great ease.
They waved hello with slippery fins,
While crabs threw shells for fun-filled wins.

Each wave that lapped embraced a laugh,
As dolphins danced in a playful half.
They took to jumps and flips galore,
Making waves right up to the shore.

But watch your step, the tides might play,
And sweep your sandwich far away.
With salty breeze and chuckling crests,
The sea's great joy never takes a rest.

Caresses of the Coastal Breeze

The breeze tickled kites high in the air,
While kids screamed loudly with carefree flair.
Sandcastles crumble as they do shout,
"Hey! Watch that wave! It's coming out!"

Seagulls giggle, swooping down low,
Stealing fries with a mischievous bow.
They chuckle while making their quick retreat,
Leaving behind no trace but defeat.

Tide pools bubble, snails roll in style,
Waving at surfers who bobbed for a while.
With each little splash, a playful grudge,
The sea gives everyone a light nudge.

And behold! The beach ball came to play,
Bouncing around in an awkward way.
It rolled into trouble, but what a thrill,
As laughter took over the salty hill.

Chasing Shadows Over the Deep

Bubbles popped up from below, so neat,
As fish played tag, quick on their feet.
They dodged and weaved with a splashy cheer,
While octopuses waved their arms in leer.

Bright sun shone down, a bright golden glee,
As crabs crawled sideways with utmost spree.
"Catch me if you can!" they dared in jest,
While plankton threw a wild, tiny fest.

Sunbathers giggled, shook sand from their toes,
Watching the scene with joyous repose.
A sea turtle wearing a party hat,
Scooted by, flipping just like a acrobat.

Along came a wave, big and grand,
Who knew that mischief was part of the plan.
It tumbled and giggled, rolled for a while,
Leaving beachgoers with sandy smiles.

shards of Light and Memory

The sun dipped low, painting skies bright,
As laughter erupted with sheer sunlight.
A crab declared, "Today's a delight!"
While jellyfish twirled in colorful flight.

Kids in the surf, splashing about,
Skipping along with a screeching shout.
Each wave brought whispers of silly dreams,
And sparkled like magic, or so it seems.

Beach balls collide, it's a game of fate,
As laughter builds, it feels like fate.
The waves laugh back, tickling toes,
And seagulls swoop by with daring shows.

As sun melts down, the shadows grow long,
The sea sings softly a soothing song.
In the end, the memories gleam so bright,
What a riot at dusk, pure delight!

Waves of Contemplation

A wave rolled in with a quirky grin,
It whispered jokes that made me spin.
I laughed so hard, I lost my hat,
A seagull swooped in, and off he sat.

The tide was in on silly schemes,
It played with boats and stole their dreams.
With every splash, it seemed to say,
"Join the fun, don't drift away!"

Bubbles danced like they knew a tune,
While crabby crabs sang out of tune.
I chuckled as they made a mess,
The sea's own goofy, fishy jest.

In this vast blue with mirth galore,
I found such joy upon the shore.
With each high tide, my heart did swell,
Another chuckle, never a dull spell.

Mirror of the Deep

Beneath the waves, where fish all play,
I met a dolphin who joked all day.
He told me tales of his frothy friends,
And all the mischief that never ends.

A crab in a tux, stepping with flair,
Said, "Join my dance, if you dare!"
I tripped and fell; oh what a sight,
We laughed till the sun began to bite.

Jellyfish boogied, glowing so bright,
While sea turtles chuckled at my plight.
In bubbles and giggles, the ocean sighed,
Its shimmering surface couldn't hide.

What truths are found where laughter flows,
In depths so silly, where humor grows?
With fishy puns and bubbles that gleam,
The sea's a dream that tickles the beam.

Tides of Thought

As the tide sways, so do my thoughts,
Floating like boats that life has brought.
Some days they splash with joy so bright,
Others drift quietly, out of sight.

A starfish asked, "Why walk on land?"
"I'd rather swim! Come take my hand!"
We giggled as we danced on shells,
Telling sea tales that no one tells.

With each reflection, a chuckle to spare,
The ocean's riddle, a whimsical dare.
I pondered deep, then splashed it away,
With fishy grins and splashes of play.

So next time you see the sea's vast blue,
Remember to smile, it's laughing at you.
For in its embrace of waves and delight,
Lies joy hidden, oh what a sight!

Secrets Beneath the Surface

What secrets swirl in the ocean's swell?
A fish with glasses said, "I'll tell!"
He winked and giggled, fins in a flap,
While seaweed joined in for a chat.

A clam complained, "Why's it so deep?"
"Because the mermaids have dreams to keep!"
They sang and splashed, such a funny hoot,
With octopus arms that danced in a suit.

Down below, where laughter flows light,
They joked about sharks, quite the fright!
"We're friends, you see, they just want a snack,
But they always come for a laugh and a quack!"

So dive in deep and roll with the tide,
Where silly fish tales take you for a ride.
Secrets of joy in the bubbles that rise,
The ocean's humor is quite the surprise!

Chasing the Horizon's Embrace

My friend jumped in, splashing around,
Thought he was a dolphin, but look who's drowned!
With flippers of noodles, he flailed in delight,
Chasing a seagull that took off in flight.

The waves all giggled, dancing with glee,
As he tried to surf on a buoyant sea spree.
A splash and a crash, he rides a small wave,
Declared he's the king of this watery cave.

His laughter echoed, flippers on toes,
While sandcastles crumbled, oh how it shows!
He built a grand tower that tipped in a twist,
Now he's just a sandman, lost in a mist.

So here's to the ocean, both wild and free,
Where every splash story is a hit for me.
With waves as our jokers, we'll surf and we'll play,
Chasing horizon's jokes, come join in the fray!

Tides that Whisper Secrets

The tide told a secret, but I can't quite hear,
It chuckled and bubbled, then splashed up my beer.
I asked for advice on my sunburned nose,
But it just laughed, like a ticklish rose.

Seagulls joined in with their cawing delight,
They dance like they're grooving, oh what a sight!
One tried to steal fries, then flew off so quick,
Wonder if they're training to become a slick trick?

The driftwood's a poet, in logs it does write,
With scribbles of laughter, it glows in the night.
It tells tales of crabs with their sideways prance,
And jellyfish doing the wiggly dance.

So next time you wander where the tides play,
Listen close, my friend, to what they might say.
With humor and wisdom from the rippling foam,
You'll find laughter and joy in the sea's salty home!

Colors of Dusk in Aquifer Streams

When the sun takes a dive, the streams feel so bright,
They giggle and shimmer, a colorful sight.
Fish don their evening gowns, ready to sway,
As the watercolors blend in a playful ballet.

The minnows are gossiping, swirling about,
"Did you hear that joke?" they giggle and shout.
A turtle joins in, his shell like a shield,
Claiming, "I'm the best at hiding my field!"

Jellybean seaweeds dance in the flow,
"Let's throw a party!" they cheerily glow.
With shells as fine hats and stones as the cake,
They sing with the bubbles for fun's own sake.

So linger by dusk, where the soft currents gleam,
Join in the laughter, live out your dream.
The colors of twilight will tickle your cheek,
In aquifer streams, they're at their peak!

Threads of Silver in Twilit Waters

At twilit hour, when day meets the night,
The fish wear their pajamas; it's quite a sight!
With threads of silver, they glide with such grace,
Swapping fishy jokes in their watery space.

A starfish just winked, with a smile so wide,
"Who needs an ocean when you've got the tide?"
The crabs played rock-paper-scissors for fun,
"Best out of three? I'm the king, I just won!"

The moon hangs above in a shimmering glow,
While angelfish sparkle, "Let's put on a show!"
They twirl and they twist in a theatrical way,
Even the barnacles joined in the play.

So if you're down by the water's soft gleam,
Remember the laughter, the joy, and the dream.
In the twilight's embrace, where waters are bright,
The threads of silver dance with sheer delight!

Secrets of the Tempest

A seagull stole my sandwich there,
With a sneaky swoop, just like a hare.
Fish are laughing, bubbles burst,
While the crab plays tag, that little jerk!

The waves are giggling, so well they sway,
Jellyfish dance like they've found a way.
I try to join, but trip on sand,
And end up splashing, it's not what I planned!

There's a fish with glasses, reading a book,
Claiming it's magic, come take a look!
I asked him to share, but he flipped a fin,
And with a wink, he swam off with a grin.

The sun sets low, painting skies bright,
Crabs throw a party, it's quite the sight.
While I'm here bumbled, tangled in seaweed,
They sing and they dance, oh, to be freed!

Light Dancers on Liquid Glass

In the shallows where sunbeams play,
Tiny turtles groove the day away.
A starfish with moves, it's quite a sight,
Breakdancing right in the pale moonlight!

Octopi wear hats, looking quite dapper,
While squid squirt ink like it's a caper.
Jellybeans floating, they bump and roll,
With the rhythm of currents, they're on a stroll!

The coral chorus sings in delight,
As sea cucumbers take their flight.
Fish in tuxedos believe they're the best,
But the clownfish chortle and outshine the rest!

With bubbles as confetti, the party's ablaze,
Who knew the sea could hold such a craze?
I splash my feet, trip on a log,
And the whole crowd giggles, oh what a fog!

Shimmering Echoes of Solstice

When the sun smiles wide, the waves tickle toes,
Kites sailing high, where the sweet wind blows.
Fish in sunglasses throw shade on their fins,
While crabs stage mock battles and laugh at their sins.

A dolphin dashes, flips in pure glee,
Claiming, 'This trick? Bet you can't see!'
But I'm just here, tripping on my own feet,
And wave after wave knocks me off my seat!

Seashells converse, whispering secrets of old,
While seaweed wiggles, shimmering like gold.
A conch shell booms, giving out a loud shout,
But everyone just giggles, "What's that about?"

Finally the sun dips, casting shadows so tall,
With laughter and splashes, we dance in the hall.
Though soaked to the bone, I can't help but grin,
These echoes of laughter are where the fun begins!

Moments in the Wake of Waves

Waves crash and splatter, it's messy, no doubt,
A fish in a top hat looks around, and shouts.
Seagulls are stealing the last of the fries,
They dive with such flair, it's a birdie surprise!

Drifting on swells, my floatie's my throne,
But a big wave crashes, and I'm all alone.
Paddling frantically, I'm thrown off course,
While sea stars point, giggling with remorse!

Sandcastles tumble, oh, what a sight,
As the tide rolls in, claiming the night.
But the clams are all cheering, 'Hey, join our band!'
While I just chuckle, buried deep in the sand!

Stars twinkle down, as the tide ebbs away,
The laughter lingers, oh, what a display!
In these carefree moments, I find such delight,
In the quirky little world where sea life ignites!